ANIMAL JOURNEYS

Migrating with the Humpback Whale

Thessaly Catt

PowerKiDS press

New York

Published in 2011 by The Rosen Publishing Group, Inc.
29 East 21st Street, New York, NY 10010

First Edition

Editor: Amelie von Zumbusch
Book Design: Ashley Burrell

Photo Credits: Cover, p. 4 © www.iStockphoto.com/Josh Friedman; p. 5 Eastcott Momatiuk/Getty Images; p. 6 © www.iStockphoto.com/John Pitcher; p. 7 © www.iStockphoto.com/Robert Plotz; p. 8 © www. iStockphoto.com/Adam Troyer; p. 9 (top) © www.iStockphoto.com/Jan Kratochvila; p. 9 (bottom) © www. iStockphoto.com/Jan-Dirk Hansen; pp. 10–11, 20 (bottom) © www.iStockphoto.com/Liz Leyden; pp. 12 (top), 16 Shutterstock.com; p. 12 (bottom) © Masa Ushioda/age fotostock; p. 14 © www.iStockphoto. com/Xavier Marchant; p. 15 (top) © www.iStockphoto.com/Brett Atkins; p. 15 (bottom) Alexander Safonov/Getty Images; p. 17 iStockphoto/Thinkstock; p. 18 David Tipling/Getty Images; p. 19 © www. iStockphoto.com/Earle Keatley; p. 20 (top) © www.iStockphoto.com/Edzard de Ranitz; p. 21 Justin Sullivan/Getty Images; p. 22 Nancy Ostertag/Getty Images.

Library of Congress Cataloging-in-Publication Data

Catt, Thessaly.
 Migrating with the humpback whale / by Thessaly Catt. — 1st ed.
    p. cm. — (Animal journeys)
 Includes index.
 ISBN 978-1-4488-2543-1 (library binding) — ISBN 978-1-4488-2670-4 (pbk.) —
 ISBN 978-1-4488-2671-1 (6-pack)
 1. Humpback whale—Juvenile literature. 2. Humpback whale—Migration—Juvenile literature. I. Title.
 QL737.C424C38 2011
 599.5'251568—dc22
                               2010027076

Manufactured in the United States of America

CPSIA Compliance Information: Batch #WW11PK: For Further Information contact Rosen Publishing, New York, New York at 1-800-237-9932

Contents

A Humpback's Journey 4

All the World's Oceans 6

Flippers and Flukes 8

Finding Food and Staying Warm 10

The Humpback Whale's Migration 12

Splashing and Singing 14

Mothers and Calves 16

Hungry Humpbacks 18

Studying Humpbacks 20

Humpbacks in Trouble 22

Glossary 23

Index 24

Web Sites 24

A Humpback's Journey

Have you ever seen birds flying south for the winter? These birds are migrating. A migration is a journey that some animals make. Animals often migrate to find food, warm weather, or a place to have babies. Though birds may be the best-known

This humpback whale is in the waters off French Polynesia. Many humpbacks spend their winters there.

In the summer, humpback whales make their way to cooler waters. This humpback is swimming in waters off Antarctica.

migrating animals, many animals migrate. One of the most interesting migrating animals is the huge humpback whale.

Each year, humpback whales around the world migrate between **polar** waters in the summer and **tropical** waters in the winter. Their **route** between polar and tropical waters can be over 3,000 miles (4,800 km) long. This means that some humpback whales travel over 300,000 miles (480,000 km) in their lives.

All the World's Oceans

Humpback whales live in all the world's oceans. However, scientists divide the world's humpback whales into three main groups, or **populations**. One large population of humpback whales lives in the North Atlantic Ocean. There are also populations of humpbacks in the North Pacific Ocean and in the oceans of the Southern **Hemisphere**.

Many of the humpbacks from the North Pacific population come to Alaska's Frederick Sound to feed in the summer.

Most humpback whales travel to warm tropical waters in the winter to **mate** and have babies, called calves. In the summer, they migrate to cooler polar waters to hunt for food. However, scientists think that the humpback whales that live in the northern Indian Ocean do not migrate.

The whales that spend the summer in Alaska's Frederick Sound migrate to the waters off Hawaii for the winter. This whale is off the Hawaiian island of Maui.

Flippers and Flukes

Humpback whales are **mammals**. As all mammals do, they breathe air. Humpbacks swim up to the ocean's surface to breathe. They breathe through the two blowholes on top of their heads.

When whales, such as these humpbacks, come up to breathe, they let out a stream of air that produces mist. The stream is called a spout.

Humpbacks have smooth bodies. They are generally black on top and white on the bottom. They are about 50 feet (15 m) long, with flippers that can reach more than 15 feet (5 m) long. Humpbacks also have wide tails, called flukes.

Humpbacks arch, or bend, their backs when they dive deep underwater. Their way of bending their backs earned the whales their name.

Humpbacks have the longest flippers of any kind of whale. Their flippers are also known as pectoral fins.

Instead of teeth, humpbacks have baleen plates. They filter their food through their baleen. This means they can swallow a lot of food at one time because they do not have to chew.

Finding Food and Staying Warm

Humpback whales migrate to their polar feeding grounds each summer because there is lots of food there for the humpbacks to eat. However, humpbacks do not have enough body fat to stay warm in polar waters during the winter. They must migrate back to tropical waters for the winter and spring. These warm waters are also where they mate and have babies.

Did you know that when it is summer in the Northern Hemisphere, it is winter in the Southern Hemisphere? This means that humpbacks in the Northern Hemisphere migrate to their feeding grounds when humpbacks in the Southern Hemisphere migrate to their breeding grounds. For this reason, these two humpback populations never meet.

The polar waters where humpbacks spend the summer have many melting glaciers, or masses of ice. This makes for rich waters that hold lots of food for the whales.

The Humpback Whale's Migration

Many humpbacks in the North Pacific population breed and have their calves in the waters off Hawaii.

Migrating humpback whales can swim as fast as 16 miles per hour (26 km/h).

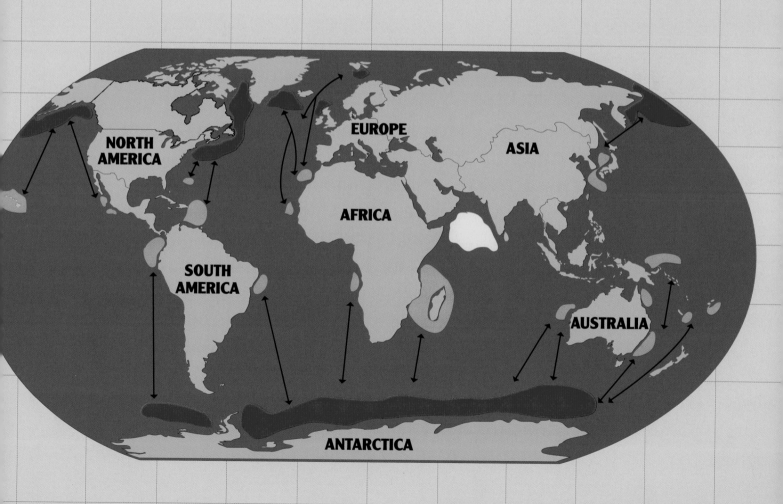

Map Key

- Breeding Grounds
- Feeding Grounds
- Possible Year-Round Indian Ocean Population

Below: The arrows here connect the breeding and feeding grounds that humpback populations most often use. Scientists are still studying the North Indian Ocean humpbacks, but they think that they do not migrate.

NORTH AMERICA

EUROPE

ASIA

AFRICA

SOUTH AMERICA

AUSTRALIA

ANTARCTICA

Splashing and Singing

Humpback whales do not stick together closely when they are migrating. However, groups of humpbacks catch fish together in the summer. In the winter, groups of up

Humpbacks are huge, but they move through the water with great skill and ease.

to 20 male humpbacks gather around one female when it is time to mate. These males try to **attract** the female by jumping out of the water or splashing with their flippers or flukes. Scientists think humpbacks use these **behaviors** to **communicate** with each other, too.

Humpback whales breach, or use their tails to send all or most of their bodies out of the water. Then they land with big splashes.

The male humpbacks in the same waters sing the same song. The song changes a bit from year to year, though.

Scientists think that male humpbacks may communicate with other humpbacks or try to find mates by singing. Humpback songs are long strings of sounds that the whales make underwater. One song can last for as long as 30 minutes.

Mothers and Calves

Mother humpbacks take good care of their calves. They almost always swim close to their calves.

After humpback whales mate, the female humpback is pregnant for about a year before her calf is born. Female humpbacks generally have one calf every two or three years. Calves are born in the winter, after humpbacks have migrated to their breeding grounds. Newborn calves are generally around 10 to 15 feet (3–5 m) long. They can weigh up to 1 ton (907 kg)! Like other baby mammals, calves nurse, or drink their mothers' milk.

Calves stay with their mothers for almost a year. Young humpbacks keep growing until they are about 10 years old. Humpbacks can start having babies when they are between 6 and 10 years old. They can live for up to 50 years.

Mothers and calves are often the last humpbacks to leave the winter breeding grounds and migrate to their summer feeding grounds.

Hungry Humpbacks

Adult humpbacks catch and eat food only in the summer, at their feeding grounds. In the winter, they do not need to eat because they have stored fat, called blubber, in their bodies. Humpbacks often eat small sea creatures, such as krill and

These small animals are krill. Though krill are only about 2 inches (5 cm) long, they are an important food for huge humpback whales.

These humpback whales are off the coast of Alaska. They are making a bubble net to catch a kind of fish called herring.

plankton. They also eat fish, such as anchovies, cod, sardines, and mackerel. Humpbacks may eat up to 1.5 tons (1 t) of food in a day.

One way humpback whales hunt is by making bubble nets. A group of humpbacks will surround a group of fish. Then, the whales swim in circles and blow bubbles of air through their blowholes. This traps the fish in a net of bubbles.

Studying Humpbacks

Scientists study humpback whales for many reasons, such as to learn more about their migration or how they communicate. One way that scientists can tell different humpbacks apart is by their flukes. Each whale's fluke is different, like a person's fingerprint. **Identifying** whales by their flukes lets scientists track different humpbacks around the world.

Here, you can see the differences in shape and black-and-white patterns on the flukes of two humpback whales.

Other people besides scientists like to watch humpbacks as well. Many people enjoy whale watching, or going on boat rides to see whales swim, jump, and splash in the water. Humpback whale watching is well liked in many places, such as Alaska and Hawaii.

These girls spotted a humpback in California's Sacramento River. Humpbacks sometimes get lost and swim up rivers. When this happens, people often try to help them return to the sea.

Humpbacks in Trouble

Humpback whales do not have many animal **predators**. They are more often killed by ocean **pollution**, ships, and fishing gear than by other animals. Between the seventeenth and twentieth centuries, many people hunted humpbacks. Humpback whales became **endangered** during this time. Today, though, hunting humpbacks is against the law in many countries.

Scientists worry that humpback populations might get smaller because of problems like pollution. However, people are working to save these incredible migrating animals. Scientists, whale watchers, and others look forward to learning more about humpback whales in the years to come.

There are many groups that work to make the oceans safe for humpbacks and other whales.

Glossary

attract (uh-TRAKT) To cause people, animals, or things to want to be near you.

behaviors (bee-HAY-vyurz) Ways to act.

communicate (kuh-MYOO-nih-kayt) To share facts or feelings.

endangered (in-DAYN-jerd) In danger of no longer living.

hemisphere (HEH-muh-sfeer) Half of Earth.

identifying (eye-DEN-tuh-fy-ing) Telling what something is.

mammals (MA-mulz) Warm-blooded animals that have backbones and hair, breathe air, and feed milk to their young.

mate (MAYT) To come together to make babies.

polar (POH-lur) Having to do with the places around the North Pole and the South Pole.

pollution (puh-LOO-shun) Manmade wastes that hurt Earth's air, land, or water.

populations (pop-yoo-LAY-shunz) Groups of animals or people living in the same place.

predators (PREH-duh-terz) Animals that kill other animals for food.

route (ROOT) The path a person or animal takes to get somewhere.

tropical (TRAH-puh-kul) Having to do with the warm parts of Earth that are near the equator.

Index

A

air, 8, 19

B

babies, 4, 7, 10, 17
blowholes, 8, 19
bodies, 9, 18

C

calves, 7, 16–17

F

flippers, 9, 15
fluke(s), 9, 15, 20
food, 4, 7, 9–10, 18–19

M

males, 15
mammals, 8, 17

N

North Atlantic Ocean, 6
North Pacific Ocean, 6

P

pollution, 22
population(s), 6, 11, 22
predators, 22

R

route, 5

S

scientists, 6–7, 15, 20–22
Southern Hemisphere, 6, 11
summer, 5, 7, 10–11, 14, 18
surface, 8

T

tails, 9

W

water(s), 5, 7, 10, 15, 21
weather, 4
winter, 4–5, 7, 10–11, 14, 16, 18

Web Sites

Due to the changing nature of Internet links, PowerKids Press has developed an online list of Web sites related to the subject of this book. This site is updated regularly. Please use this link to access the list:

www.powerkidslinks.com/anjo/humpback/